A Cup of Tea and a Tickle of Rum

A Cup of Tea and a Tickle of Rum

India Hosten-Hughes

Speaking Tongues Press.

A Cup of Tea and a Tickle of Rum
First published 2016 by Speaking Tongues Press

Harley House Publications
Unit 10421
PO Box 6945
London
W1A 6US

Cover design by Nathan Garwood

ISBN: Hardback - 978-0-9955373-0-9
ISBN: Paperback - 978-0-9955373-1-6
ISBN: E-Book - 978-0-9955373-3-0

www.harleyhousepub.co.uk
info@harleyhousepub.co.uk

STP
SPEAKING
TONGUES
PRESS

Dedication

I would like to dedicate this book to my late grandmother, who was the most influential role model in my life and has been my constant muse.

To my mother, who sparked the fire that burns inside me to write and explore all of my creative identity.

Thank you. x

To a Tea

To drink my English tea
I have a selfish teapot
Earl Grey, Tetley's, PG
I like to drink the lot.

Jacob's Cream Crackers;
Buttered, jammed and spread
Shortbread, cookies, a slice of cake
Maybe hard dough bread?

Honey, lemon, a ginger slice
Got a cold? Add some spice
A shot of rum to warm the chest
Two shots for extra rest.

I love a cup of tea,
As long as it looks like me.

(Just a dash of milk)

Table of Contents

Food Porn

Diabetes

Hello sugar
Wa' gwarnin' sweetness
I like chocolate
Reese's pieces
Candy apple
Apple bottom
Juicy melons
Mangos and plums
Caramel macchiato, frappuccino, latte skin
Waar'um me good-as sugar dumpling
Honey milk
Toffee cream
My golden nugget sugar dream
Birthday cake
Cream of the crop
Crème de la crème
iHop.

This is how people greet me.
I think they want to eat me.

Soul Food

Nostalgia hits the heart when Ma or Grandma
cooks. The smell of hard work, love and
seasoning decorates the house: coating the
wallpaper of each room with a sweet and
savoury fragrance – a taste of a foreign home.

Family bonds over plates piled high. Laughter
and prayers entice reminiscent conversations
of cleared up memories.

Full-bellied murmurs groan at the table as the
overeaters undo belts and trouser buttons.
The children laugh at the uncles; the aunts
dish out dessert.

The cousins play cards as the elders play
dominos; slapping hands down on tables,
knees and thighs. Spirits lifted high.

Ma and Grandma sit at the head of the table;
thick smiles and closed eyes, their heads lean
back listening to a room filled with chatter and
laughter – they pray.

They thank the Lord for the food.
We thank the Lord for the hands that made it.

Sweet Sugar Dumpling

With eyes like honey and skin like tea
Not even sugar dumpling coulda sweeter dan
me

Skin sarf like grapes
And me juicy like melon
Teeth them pure and hair like lion

Big man waarn ask me, me name
Say I look like foreign
I say foreign be my name
Dem waarn a piece of my caramel skin
But dem look like old cruff Shabba Rank'in

Mind like axe
Ears hot like fire
Eyes brighter than the hottest furnace pyre
Riper than berry
Brown sugar toffee
Me have one hell of a shapely body

Me say, no body coulda sweeter dan me
With eyes like honey and skin like tea
Not even bullah cake coulda spicy dan me
Favor encona, scotch bonnet pepper

But I am not groceries
I am not food
I am not a treat, just for you
I am not a midnight snack
Or your sweetly sin
– Even if I look like a sugar dumpling.

Mash-up menu

Full English

 Two eggs
Bacon and beans
Plantain
Fried dumpling
And leafy greens

Sunday English Roast

 Chicken
Yorkshire pudding
Coleslaw
Mac and Cheese
Rice and peas
Potato salad
Fruit punch
Guinness punch
 Carrot Juice

My mother never knows what to feed me
Me and my mash-up food
She slaps everything on my plate
My English-Jamaican menu.

Simplicit-tea

I pretend to like the taste of wine
Fermented grapes set over time
But I'd rather have a shot of rum
Or darker means to have some fun

Wine is free and so I drink
At tables filled with faces pink
I sit and smile
Dressed in style
Wondering what the faces think

I'd rather be at home instead
Dressed, ready and prepped for bed
A bubble bath to set the mood
New pyjamas; silk and smooth

You'll find me on a Friday night
With a cup of tea, wrapped up tight.

Home
Grown

Identity Politics

I was told I was Black as soon as I could identify differences, like understanding there are girls and boys. To be Black meant that I had coloured skin, but that didn't define who I was.

The first time I consciously acknowledged race was the first time I met my grandfather on a beach in Grenada. Stood before me was a White man with green eyes and gelled-slicked, jet-black hair and a gold chain around his neck. He spoke with an island accent; native to the tongue, the culture – the life. When I looked at this man, I didn't see my grandfather. I couldn't see past that he was a White man and I was Black. I couldn't wait to go to school and tell the kids that I was mixed raced; excited that I was unique and different. But they didn't care, my school was equally as diverse I – we played football with tennis balls on the hockey court.

With secondary school came the clash of the clans: Blacks vs. Blacks/ Africans vs. West Indians in a battle of who was more civil and less of a barbarian: a battle of culture, customs and food, concocted by systems centuries

before our time as we acted on divisions
created to loosen our bonds and strengthen
our weaknesses.

I sat on the sidelines watching the races.
Mixed-raced kids with Black dads and White
mums called mixed-raced kids with Black
mums and White dads backwards.

My mother told me I'm Black, not only
because that's how White people will see me,
but because I should be proud of my ancestry.
Mixed-race kids are Black, yet on demographic
surveys they are dual heritage and I am Other
(please define).

Constantly asked 'what are you? Where are
you from?' Somalis assume I am Somali and
speak to me in Somali. West Indians and
Africans fetishize me because I have light skin
with light eyes, wondering what exotic mixes
lie in me. Told by Black people I can't be fully
Black because I don't have Black features. For
many summers I laid in the sun wishing to get
darker, but my red skin only resembled the
complexion of Sri Lankans.

In a pro-identity society, pro-British, pro-African, pro-Caribbean, I cannot easily fit into one like slipping on a shoe and say 'this is my identity!' Nawal El Saadawi taught me, 'to be mixed blood, is to be rich'. So I embrace every part of me that stretches far and wide like the branches of a tree or the streams of the Nile.

I am culturally rich, owning every part of me that exists. Although my blood is mixed, together I am Black and where I was born makes me British – It's nothing more than identity politics.

Pretty for a Black Girl

The other day I was told I was pretty for a Black girl. A young Black man thought this was a good enough compliment. I had only ever seen such stupidity on Twitter when other girls had mentioned that this had happened to them – I thought about it. But I wasn't quick enough to release my wit and state that he was ugly for a Black man. All I could do was walk away and think about it.

Speaking to another guy about the essence of blackness, he told me, 'I only like Black girls with natural hair' as I sat with my twist-out looking at him. He said, 'every Black person's hair is beautiful, why do some girls wear weave? Natural hair is prettier to me.'

He didn't know how I rolled, but assumed that my bantu twist-out wasn't just a rebellious 'do' against systematic oppression but of all things non-Black, not realising that my grandfather, aunts, friends and close relatives are White and mixed-raced and that as much as I revel in my Black magic, I embrace my diversity.

So I turned and looked at this man. I smiled a coy sweet smile, sipped my tea slow and said,

'Who the hell thinks about you? All we are trying to do is go a day without taking a day-out to do our barnet. Quick things, fling on a wig and rock it. Ain't nobody got time to be messing, arm flexing, hair follicle stretching to please you!'

He questioned my position as a young Black woman who usually rocks natural hair. I said,

'Dude, it's every day scatty don't judge me. Just because my hair is natural on Monday, by Wednesday it could be weaved up pony, in a fortnight it could be trackless keep it braid-wavy. So never ever think that by my hair you know me. Don't get me wrong, I myself prefer natural hair than weave, doesn't mean that, come birthdays, weddings and New Years Eve that 1B three pack, Expressions extensions is not in me. I don't have to look prettier because I have straight hair 12 inches longer than my own, but that effort to maintain natural hair is resistance training on it's own. Deep lie in our African roots are braids and extensions, so don't tell me that my culture is appropriating.'

My aunt and I were watching X factor, and there was by Simon's side as per usual Sinitta. My aunt watched Sinitta make a fool of herself in her fig leaves and twigs. My aunt remarked,

'She has no Black in her. She can't relate to Black people'. I asked my aunt in a nonchalant way, 'what is black but the pigmentation of ones skin, the DNA passed down by kin.'

She looked at me in that Black aunt way like to say 'India, shut up. You know what I mean.' But me being me, I pressed on.

Black is the signifier of our race but we don't reflect the dark connotations and representation of the blackness on our skin. A person's culture does not define their race or whom they identify with. A person's identity is who they are individually. As Black people, we have multiple cultures and customs globally. Black is not just one culture, Black is a united face.

Proud Fro

The pitter-patter on my window
The howling of the wind
The rushing power flooding down
Letting the cool breeze in.

I want to go outside
I want to soak it in.
But I have a Black girl's fro
My hair would turn to tight, tight curls.
The effort to comb out the shrinkage
The force to remove all knots
To bring back the power and life of my bush
I guess I better not.

I will continue to look outside my window
I will watch and listen from inside.
As much as I want to dance in the rain
My fro has too much pride.

When you look in the mirror, what do you see?

When I look in the mirror what do I see?
I see a brown girl staring back at me
With eyes like honey
And skin like tea
I see a brown girl staring back at me.

When I look in the mirror, what do I see?
I see a brown girl as pretty as can be
With tight black curls
And voluptuous curves
I see a brown girl staring back at me.

When I look in the mirror, what do I see?
I see a young woman staring back me
With a strong mind
And magic in her eyes
I see a brown girl staring back at me.

When I look in the mirror, what do I see?
I see mothers, daughters, sisters and friends
I see confidence and strength
I see women of power and success.

When I look in the mirror, what do I see?
I see a brown girl staring back at me.
When I look in the mirror what do I see?
I see you. I see me.

Tolerated

We love to talk about diversity. Excited that
Samantha from around the corner had a baby
with a Black man. You compliment the child's
golden skin, her thick curly hair and bright
brown eyes. Yet neglect to accept that this
child is still Black, just fair.

You are quick to shout 'look how tolerant and
accepting we are of other people's ethnicities.
We have a Black child in our community,
occasionally celebrating inclusivity. Look at
our diversity.'

We pick and choose who gets immunity to live
in our towns and cities, not wanting too many
ethnicities decreasing the value of our property
– but just enough to help with our economy.

In controversial conversations, accusations
on racism, discussing forms of discrimination,
you quickly defend yourself in the situation by
stating – you have a 'Black friend'.

You want to say the 'N' word, not because
you're racist, but for the freedom without guilt.
So you sing rap songs and Black music as
terms of endearment – excuses.

You boast about school days; wearing your hair in braids, going to Jamaica on holiday – and eating jerk chicken. You love reggae and have a Bob Marley ashtray – as if this is Black living.

You make jokes with your friends about Black men, degrading them to stereotypes of big black innuendos; creating erotic fantasies. And yet again, you refuse to acknowledge the racial issues that exist around them as many struggle to find jobs, build businesses and receive the same opportunities as you.

Another Black man shot on the TV. A video showing extreme police brutality, as you sit with your Black friend awkwardly - waiting to defend yourself.

You are confused by why you should support Black Lives Matter when All Lives Matter, as people die all over the world – in constant devastation. But you understand that feminism is for all; founded for female equality and later evolving to gender unity - And still, you can not fathom Black Lives Matter.

For All Lives Matter, Muslim women are still racially attacked here in our hometown. You

say you are tolerant, yet can't stand how many
Asians – have taken over businesses and
increasing in population.

You eat Indian and Chinese takeaways and
Kebabs on Fridays. Your doctor is African
and his name Ajaye – you find it difficult to
pronounce so you call him Dr. A.

'I'm not a racist but...' You're fed up with all the
different races. No longer the most prominent
face. You tolerate ethnicities like tolerating a
child that's not yours. You lack patience when
you show them acceptance and kindness – yet
they don't listen to you despite this.

For such a tolerant society, why are we still
struggling with equality?

Foreign Memories

Forgotten land

From when last you reach home
– English girl
You don't know 'bout your roots
You just know where you've grown.
You drink English tea in the morning, noon
and night
But you don't know anything about your
heritage's plight.

When last you think to call abroad
– English girl
You read plenty foreign books
But your education is flawed.
You read about dead white men and
their history
All you know of yours is black slavery.

English girl,
Do you know who you are?
Do you know where you come from?
That you belong afar?
You fit in well
Speak fluently
But what do you class as your identity?

Brown-Eyed Girl

Brown-eyed girl
Pretty brown-eyed girl
Swerve her hips
And twirl her curls

Brown-eyed girl
Pretty brown-eyed girl
Come mek me show you
De ways of de worl'

Brown-eyed girl
Oh brown-eyed girl
Come mek me feel yuh
And hol' ya close

Brown eye girl
Pretty brown-eyed girl
Ya pretty brown eyes
Will send me to jail

The wolves are not puppies
Neither cute nor fluffy
Dey are dangerous animals
And you are their prey
Brown-eyed girl
Mek sure you – run away

Brown-eyed girl
Pretty brown-eyed girl
Tek care of your body
Tek care of yourself

Brown-eyed girl
Little brown-eyed girl
Watch for the wolves
And them low bent tails

If I was younger and fitter
I'd be right there after ya
You mek a mans mind go crazy
Ambition lazy
Brown-eyed girl
Likkle brown-eyed girl
Tek care of your body
Tek care of yourself.

Foreigner at Home

My grandparents never spoke of Jamaica.
So adapted to the streets of England they
never looked back.
They never made plans to return home
They had new lives now and that was that.

I don't know much about Jamaica, all I know
is food.
And even then, only a small amount
– My patois sounds like a fool.

I never knew my father's parents,
They were a small island clan.
Barbados and Grenada
From what I understand.

But I know London
Croydon, my home.
To go back to my grandparents land
I'll be a foreigner at home.

Oranges

My granddad loved oranges from Jamaica. They were big and round and juicy. He would cut them in quarters and hand one to me with a napkin. We would sit in silence slurping away at the sweet sticky zest of orange juice, smiling with our orange peel grins.

My granddad loved mangos. He would buy a big crate of mangos from Jamaica. He would peel the mangos bare, slice and dice them. Chop! Chop! Chop! He would put them in a bowl and drizzle thick double cream on top. We chapped and munched and slurped away on our delicious, juicy mangos and cream.

My granddad loved patties. He bought them from Jamaica too. Whatever food he could get from Jamaica, he bought.

One day, my grandma took me to the fruit and veg market. I saw yam, plantain, strawberries, lemons, oranges and mangos. Behind the fruit and veg were granddad's favourite patties.

'Grandma...' I began, '.... we have big oranges here! And look, they have mangos too! There are granddad's patties and drinks. We have them all here. Why does granddad by them all the way from Jamaica?'

My grandma looked at me and smiled, 'good question. Maybe you should ask him when we get home'.

When we got home, granddad was there slurping away at his big Jamaican oranges.

'Granddad...' I began, 'we have big oranges here! They have mangos and strawberries and patties and plantain, they even have your favourite drink'.

Granddad put down his orange and said, 'There is no orange in the world juicier than the oranges from my grandmother's garden, no mangos sweeter than the mangos from my mothers house, no patty as flavour-some as the ones my father makes. Although they are no longer here, the oranges, mangos and patties taste like home.'

The Other Side
of Paradise

'Work in England!' Said the papers.
'Roads paved with gold!' Yelled the yeller.
People started requesting favours
When they caught wind that I'll be a h'inglish
fella.

We left old town for new hope.
We set sail on a large ship boat.
Waving our home, our family and memories
– A long farewell, goodbye.

But the yeller lied.
No pavements paved with gold
No sunshine, just wind, grey and cloudy
– Everything felt cold.

We worked cleaner jobs; janitor work
Anything that made us hurt.
The White people didn't mind
They could leave the hard work
– Behind.

We sent letters to the children back home.
They sent us pictures
– They're all alone.

We had a plan, to buy a house.
But the money that we got
Was too little to count.

We tried to save all we can
Even with our mortgage plan.
To live our life back home
We needed four jobs and a loan.

We lived with three other families
In a four bedroom house.
We worked overtime, extra time
And more.
As soon as we saved enough
We bought our own house
And bolted through the door.

We settled down in Brixton
We sent for the children back home
They came here eyes wide
To see their dreams all gone.

No sun, no sea,
Just bleak misery.

We made the best that we could
Raised our children as we should
We did what we thought was right
We worked hard for a good life.

We can't go back home
It will cost too much money,
And we are now too old.
We made our bed here, our home
In the grey-lands, in England
– All alone.

Other Words

Our People

I love our people. Our people are a proud people. We are often loud making a sound with every part of our body. We are the knee slappers, table bangers, domino dashers, hard hand clappers, patty yammers and tea curers. Tea cures everything; rum cures everything.

We are no longer slaves, but we are stuck in a cycle of disproportionate equality as young Black men and women are still subject to violence, aggression and unwelcoming behaviour with rants and chants shouting 'Go Back To Africa'. Dehumanised; we have been compared to everything from Apes to shit on a shoe. For centuries we have been beaten – and still our spirits will not be broken.

We smile, we love, we feast and we celebrate; liberated in the trance of music and dance, good food and good vibes – we live life.

We are not failures. We are not a product of our image, although our image is legend. Our image is magical and real. We are the overcomers. We have overcome.

We may choose to wear weaves and laced fronts, shaped with voluptuous curves and thick bumps. Few without fathers, but you are not fatherless. Some without mothers but you are lionesses. I love my people.

I love our people. Our people have many faces. Same race yet we all run different races. Each tone an example of their own, yet we are all still known that we come from one home.

I love our people. Fifty shades of black that never cracks and a smile that travels for miles. My people are a strong people, we may be proud and loud but I will say it loud and proud. I love my people. Our people. Black people.

Mother

She carries the weight of the world on her
shoulders
When family come over, she feeds the five
thousand
She drops her own baggage to carry their
boulders
But in her mind she's drowning

Her arms stretch far, long and wide
Covering those who need her
She marches militant strides
Paving a way for those that follow her

Her back hunches over with pain and age
Her hands darkened by oven wars
Her hair is always trained and tamed
But in her eyes is still her roar

Her feet are larger and swollen
Her glow is dimming, almost dull
Her spirit lingers on unbroken
As her hum becomes a lull.

Black Sun

Our sun once reigned
In grace and beauty
How bold and heavy was its light
As smothered clouds of grey and ash
All warmth was lost but in a night.

Howling wails filled the river's black
A path of hollow soil
Too deep the tide to ride it back
To a time of mass exhale.

A raised hand and a bowed knee
Another chalk against the board
He has come with his sword unsheathed
My eyes against the Lord

In our 8th hour, our final call
One hand has drawn a breath from all.

Easy life

Don't tell me I have it easy...

Because I got a job for being Black as a part of a diversity scheme, when the only reason that scheme exists is because of the lack of equality and fairness.

When I have to fight 2.5 times harder to get the same job with the same qualifications and experience as you.

When I have to endure listening to you complain about the texture and quality of my hair and how hard it must be as if it is your burden to bear. I relish in the malleability of each strand and the beauty of my curls, so if you don't like it you know where to go.

I am subject to fetishism in different forms. Black men ridicule and mock us as White men fantasise about dipping into our chocolate pool as if we are an exotic bowl of fondue.

Not only am I Black, I am a woman.

When I walk into an interview I suffer from anxiety, worried that the employer may not like me because of things I cannot control.

Because I live in a city so accepting, tolerant and diverse. Born and raised proud and British and yet I have still been subject to acts of racism as 'thugs' shout 'GO BACK TO YOUR OWN COUNTRY!'

Because I don't. But I am fortunate, as we all are. But to say I have it easy? Just don't.

Stole

You fear me.
My words too free from my lips
You bit my tongue
And held my breath.

You captured me.
Like a precious stone
You gazed at my wonders
My many colours
Shining bright on my own.

My strength amazed you.
Like magic
I glowed.
Disillusioned by tricks and shows
You saw my visions.
- Too strong,

You feared me.
My existence baffled you.
You broke me.
Dissecting every single part of my body
You stripped me bare
So that you could understand
What it is that I am.

And still, you fear me.
You fear what you do not know.
You fear what you stole.

About the author

India Hosten-Hughes is also known by her performance name, India Harley. India developed her skills as a writer from a young age, experimenting with a variety of formats and genres. After completing a BA Joint Honours degree in Creative Writing and English Literature, India received a full scholarship to pursue further studies and a career in publishing.

Twitter: @IndiaHarley_Q
Facebook: IndiaHostenHughes1
Instagram: India_Harley

Acknowledgements

First and foremost I would like to thank Nathan Garwood for his brilliant cover design and for going above and beyond.

I would also like to thank my supervisor Emma Tait who has been an amazing mentor by supporting and guiding me through the entire process.

Thank you to Oisin Harris who's knowledge and experience with poetry and BAME literature has been greatly appreciated whilst editing *A Cup of Tea and a Tickle of Rum.*

I would like to thank everyone who has supported my journey and encouraged me that I can do this!

Thank you.

Rum Tea Recipes

The Cure

This hot honey and lemon with a few shots of rum is the perfect recipe for colds, the flu and even hangovers. If you want a good night sleep this is perfect.

Ingredients
1/2 a lemon
3 Large tablespoons of honey
1 1/2 shot of white or dark rum
1 Cup of boiling water

Method
Boil hot water. Cut a lemon in half and squeeze one half into a cup or mug. Scoop three large tablespoons of honey into the cup. Add one and a half shots of white or dark rum. Pour boiling water into the cup and stir until honey is dissolved.

Drink whilst hot!

You can also add gingerroot to the mix, perfect for the throat and chest.

Cool Runnings

You can have this drink hot or cold, either way it is deliciously refreshing.

Ingredients
Boiling or cold water
1 Handfull of fresh mint leaves
1/2 a lemon
1/2 a lime
1 1/2 dark, spiced or white rum

Method
Slice a lemon in half and squeeze one half into a cup or mug. Fold or twist mint leaves until creased and put into the cup. Slice a lime in half and squeeze lime half into cup. Add one and a half shot of prefered rum. Add boiling water or cold water and ice.

Drink whilst hot or cold!

If you drink this cold on a nice summers day, add ice and some lemonade.